I Love You, and I Never Mean to Hurt Your Feelings

Other books by

Blue Mountain Press ™

Books by Susan Polis Schutz

Come Into the Mountains, Dear Friend
I Want to Laugh, I Want to Cry
Someone Else to Love
Yours If You Ask
Love, Live and Share
Find Happiness in Everything You Do
Don't Be Afraid to Love
To My Daughter with Love
on the Important Things in Life
To My Son with Love
Take Charge of Your Body

by Susan Polis Schutz and
Katherine F. Carson, M.D.

Warmed by Love

by Leonard Nimoy

I'm on the Way to a Brighter Day

by Douglas Richards

Anthologies:

Reach Out for Your Dreams
I Promise You My Love
A Mother's Love
A Friend Forever
You Are Always My Friend
It Isn't Always Easy
My Sister, My Friend
Thoughts of Love
Thoughts of You, My Friend
You Mean So Much to Me
Love Isn't Always Easy
Don't Ever Give Up Your Dreams
When I Think About You, My Friend
I Love You, Dad
I Keep Falling in Love with You
I Will Always Remember You
For You, My Daughter
A Lasting Friendship
I Will Love You
Through Love's Difficult Times
Always Follow Your Dreams
Though We Are Apart, Love Unites Us
Mother, I Love You Forever
I'll Be Here When You Need Me
The Best Thing in Life Is a Friend
Creeds to Live By, Dreams to Follow
Thinking of You, My Sister
My Dream Is You
Mother, Thank You for All Your Love
To My Wonderful Father from Your Loving Daughter

I Love You,
and I Never Mean
to Hurt
Your Feelings

A collection of poems
Edited by Susan Polis Schutz

Blue Mountain Press ™

Boulder, Colorado

Library of Congress Catalog Card Number: 88-71783
ISBN: 0-88396-269-1

ACKNOWLEDGMENTS appear on page 62.

Manufactured in the United States of America
First printing: September, 1988

Blue Mountain Press T.M.

P.O. Box 4549, Boulder, Colorado 80306

CONTENTS

Though It May Not Always
Seem That Way . . . I Really Do Love You

Sometimes it may not seem
that I love you
Sometimes it may not seem
that I even like you
It is at these times
that you really need to
understand me more than ever
because it is at these times
that I love you more than ever
but my feelings have been hurt
Even though I try not to
I know that I am acting cold and indifferent
It is at these times that I find it so hard
to express my feelings
Often what you have done to
hurt my feelings is so small
but when you love someone
like I love you
small things become big things
and the first thing I think about
is that you do not love me
Please be patient with me
I am trying to be more honest
with my feelings
and I am trying not to be so sensitive
but in the meantime
I think you should be very confident that
at all times, in every way possible
I love you

— Susan Polis Schutz

Sometimes I Need to Know that I Make a Difference in Your Life

Every once in a while
I start feeling a little lost,
especially when I start
thinking back to where we've been
and when I start wondering
    where we're going.

    And every now and then
I need some things from you
    that I don't always get . . .

I'd like just for us to
talk a little more
and touch a little more;
there are lots of times when
I could use a reassuring hug
    and the smile that I love to see . . .
just an occasional sign
that you're still happy with me.

I'm not asking for much . . .
    just enough to know
        from time to time
    that I make a difference.
For just knowing that
makes all the difference
    in the world to me.

— Adrian Rogers

I'm Sorry for the Times
I Hurt You with
My Stormy Moods

It's hard to explain my moods;
I don't always understand them myself.
I do know that sometimes bad moods
   sneak up on me,
and before I know it,
I'm not a very pleasant person
to be around.
And unfortunately, at those times,
very often you are around,
and I know I don't treat you very well.
I'm trying to understand myself
so I can change,
but in the meantime, I want to tell you
that I'm so sorry I hurt you.
I hope you won't lose patience with me,
   because I do love you so very much.

— Vee Watts

No Matter What, I Know We'll Make It Through

Things haven't been that easy
for us lately, but I just
want you to know . . .
that as far as I'm concerned,
we're worth every single thing
it takes to keep our smiles
and our lives together.

I love you,
and that love is more important
than any other thing
could possibly be.

And maybe things haven't been
too easy for us,
    but I promise you that
        we're going to make it through

. . . because I know how strong
        my love is,
    because I have faith in us,
    and because I've never
        known anyone as
            wonderful as you.

— Carey Martin

I Love You, and I
Never Mean to Hurt You

I hope you can
forgive me for my
faults that seem
to follow my life.
Forgive me for my
    insecurities that
have caused you
    hurt and pain.
Forgive me for my
dependence on you.
It can be hard to bear.
I love you,
and I'm sorry for
any mistakes
I have made.
But remember that
my heart needs
your smiles and laughter.
My soul needs your
friendship and love.
And I
need you.

— P. F. Heller

For Any Time I Ever
Make You Unhappy

If I ever make you unhappy,
I want you to know
that I never really mean to,
but sometimes I say or do
things without thinking,
and I later regret them.

If I ever make you feel unwanted,
please don't take it personally.
There are just times when
I need to be alone
to think . . . to dream . . .
to make decisions
that only I can make.
I don't mean to shut you out.

If I ever make you feel uneasy,
   please forgive me . . .
sometimes I say things that
   make no sense or make decisions
      that are irrational.
It usually happens out of anger
   or confusion,
      but it passes quickly —
         then I'm fine.

If ever I leave you confused
   or upset,
      please talk to me.
Misunderstandings can leave
   people hurt and frightened.
I don't ever want to endanger
   our relationship —
      it's too precious.

You are a very special person,
   and I'll always treasure
      having you in my life.

                    — Donna Marie Chesla

I'm Sorry for Getting Angry,
and I Hope You Can Forgive Me

I'm sorry for those times lately
when I'm not who I should be,
when I grow impatient and frustrated
because things don't work out.
I know that you, too,
have things on your mind,
and I have no right
   to become upset with you.
It's just hard sometimes
   to understand
   the way things go wrong,
and I wanted you to know
that I'm sorry for those times
   when I become harsh
   and angry with you.
I hope you can understand
   and forgive me.

— Bethanie Jean Brevik

There's no one I'd rather spend
forever with . . . than you

One of the most valuable lessons we
can learn from life is this:

That, try as we might,
   we will never have all the answers.
We can wonder for the rest of our days
      whether we are doing the right thing . . .
         continuing in the best relationship,
         and following the best paths
            towards tomorrow,
but no one is ever going to
         answer those questions for us.

We both may have wonderings
of what to do
and curiosities of what's to come.
Time will help us with the results,
but more than any one thing,
it's up to us — and to the love
we have for each other —
to go in the right direction.

You and I sometimes wonder
about where we're headed
and whether our love will last
a lifetime through.
We may not know the answer, but
I'll tell you one thing I do know:

There's no one
I'd rather try to spend
forever with . . . than you.

— Collin McCarty

I Am Sorry, and I Love You

Sometimes I act so selfishly
that I am really ashamed
of myself
and I wonder how you could
ever forgive me
but you always do
I am so thankful that
no matter how I act
you always realize that
I love you
You are such a unique
feeling person
You demonstrate
the deepest meaning of love —
patience, understanding and caring
Once again
I am sorry
and I love you very much

— Susan Polis Schutz

When We Have Differences, Let's Be Patient with Each Other

Most relationships go through
  stressful times.
And that is why it is so important
when one of us is having
  a difficult time
to step back and realize
that what we may do or say
should not be taken personally.

If you need to draw away,
I need to remember
that it is your sorting time
and not a rejection of me.

And when I am quiet,
it does not mean I don't want
    to be with you.
It is just that I
    am thinking things through.

Let us always be patient
    with each other
and recognize and respect
        each other's individual needs.
Because if we each have
        our own inner strength,
our relationship will be stronger
and better able to withstand
    difficult times.

— Charlene A. Forsten

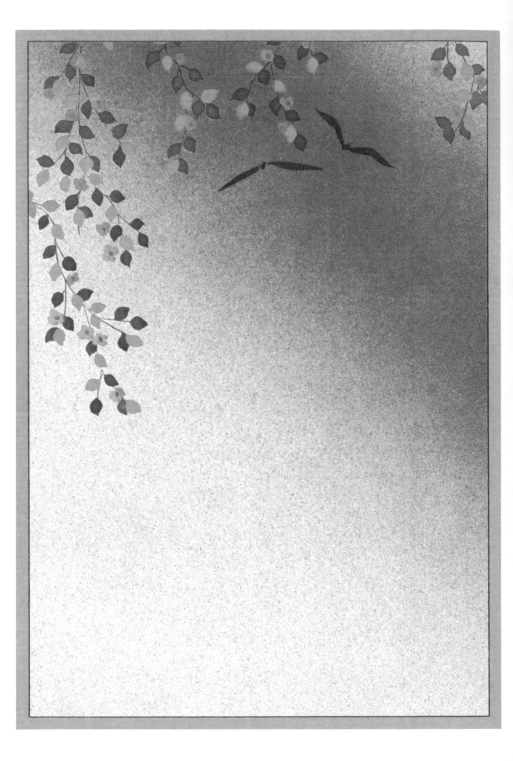

We Can Work It Out

So often, I think it's just a matter of time
before things fall into place
and our relationship works itself out.
But it seems that more than just time
     is in the way.
I can't quite explain it, but I know
     you feel it, too . . .
something isn't right between us,
and we need to talk about it.
You mean too much to me for
     our relationship to simply end.
It was so good, and we owe it
     to each other to try to bring it back.
The magic, the understanding,
are still there inside both of us.
We just have to find it again.
Things get so complicated at times,
but they're worth working at.
It's worth the time and the talking,
     the sharing.
We're worth it.
We may have to work until
     it comes easily and naturally again,
but one thing about us I am still sure of —
     I love you.

— Sharon Leigh Johnson

I Hope You Will Always
Stay in My Life

I know we've always had the ability
to really open up and talk deeply
with each other.
But lately, and for reasons
I can't explain,
I find myself feeling frightened
about what will happen with us.
I know I can't predict the future,
nor do I want to;
but sometimes I need your assurances
that everything will be all right,
and things will turn out well for us.

To think of a life without you
is to think of a life of emptiness,
filled with lonely days
and lonely thoughts.
I want to approach you
to let you know how I'm feeling,
and in doing that, I hope
we can make everything good again.
I'd really hate to lose you;
the very idea of it frightens me,
so please try and understand
my feelings about this,
because I love you
and I don't ever want to see things
change between us.

— Linda Tillmann

I Apologize for How
I've Been Acting Lately

I know that I haven't been
too compatible lately.
I can't expect you
to understand me right now,
for I'm not too sure
that I understand myself,
but the one thing that I do realize
is how important you are to me.
The rough path I have been traveling
is smoothing out,
because I have you.
You are the most positive aspect
of my life,
and your patience is the key
to realizing that, with time,
we can once again share
our smiles and secrets.
The road to resolving my problems
is leading me to happiness,
and the road to love is never ending,
as long as you continue to walk
beside me, holding my hand
as we continue our journey
towards a stronger love.

— Anne Marie Holleran

Let's Find More Time
to Share Ourselves

I wish I knew
what you are thinking about us . . .

I wish I could read your mind
instead of just trying to guess
whether you're happy with us
and whether you still
            like me . . .
Sometimes it bothers me
more than I let on that we don't
often find the time to share
our thoughts in the same way
    that we share our lives.

I wouldn't mind being closer than we are;
I wish I could feel completely at ease
    about telling you every single
    sentiment within me . . .
I think I refrain from opening up
too much because you don't seem to
    want to open up to me in return.
That's okay, though . . . because
I understand that's just the way you are.
    But I pray that you'll understand
        that there are times when
        the happiest words I could ever hear
        would be the words
            "I love you more than ever"
            . . . spoken to me by someone
            I love with all my heart
                . . . you.

— Collin McCarty

Thank You for Understanding When I'm Not Perfect

If I could love you as my heart desires,
   then my love would be perfect.
   You would never know pain
   caused by my insensitivity.
Any doubts about the depth
   of my caring
   would find rest.
I'd always say the right things
   and never disappoint you.
But I am not perfect,
   and therefore, neither is
      my love.
So instead of love without flaws,
      I have moments
   when my needs supersede your own,
   and times when I speak
      more than I listen.
I give you weakness
      instead of strength —
   hurt in place of understanding.
What I long to be for you
      and what you actually receive
      may sometimes conflict.
But if you can accept
   my imperfections,
   then you will always have
      my love.

— Paula J. Lemley

I'm Sorry that I Haven't Been Myself Lately

Please . . . bear with me;
I seem to be having one
   of those periods of time
when everything seems so bad
that I wonder if I'll ever
      be happy again.
But I know that eventually
I'll come around
and be my own cheerful self again.
It may take some time,
but bear with me,
I'll make it through.
And with your love and support
the path will be
      easier to follow.
Please . . . don't lose faith in me.
I'll be back to
being "me" again soon . . .
      I promise.

— Jane Alice Fox

If Only I Could,
I Would Take Back the Hurt

I wish we could take back
all the angry words
we threw at each other
like weapons . . .
the ones we really didn't mean
but said anyway,
because we were hurt,
confused,
and scared.
I wish I could change
the situation between us . . .
it's so uncomfortable,
and I feel like you're so
    far away from me.

I wish I could make you believe
that I still love you very much,
and that you'll always be
the most important person
in my life.
I know it will take time,
but I want to make things
    better between us,
so I will start with the
hardest part of all by saying . . .
"I'm sorry."

— Nanci Brillant

Let's Be Open
and Honest with Each Other

It's very hard sometimes to say things
    to you.
You may hear hesitation in my voice when
    there is no hesitation in my heart.
You see, I'm not always sure you will
    like what I say,
or that you will understand.
I don't want to hurt you;
I love you, and I want you to love me,
so it's important that we be open and
    honest with each other.
But it's scary sometimes, and I need
    your help to say things I need to say
        to you.
If you will help me, then I will try to
    help you when you need to say things
        to me
that you're not sure I will like.
And together, we'll learn not to be
    afraid.

— Mae Williams

I'm Sorry for the Hurt
That's Come Between Us

I know we've reached
a few impasses
in our relationship
lately,
but I think
the underlying bond
that brought us together
in the first place
is still strong enough
to weather
the troubles we're facing.
Contrary to the way
I've been acting,
I still believe in the "us"
we used to know,
and I want to see us
renew the commitment
we made to each other
and start believing
in ourselves
together
once again.

— Terry Everton

Even Though We Have
Our Disagreements,
I Always Know Our Love Is There

Too many times, it seems
we argue about everyday things
that have nothing to do
with how we feel about each other.
We say things we usually don't mean,
because we put our hearts aside
   in our anger.
Saying we're sorry doesn't always
take the pain away, but it's a start.
In spite of the pain
that our disagreements bring,
I do love you,
and I know that you love me, too.
And it's reassuring to know
that when the anger passes,
we can find our hearts again,
and the love is still there.

— Dawn M. Miller

Our Closeness Sometimes Opens Us More to Hurt

When we first stepped into each other's lives, we were so anxious to learn all about one another, and yet, because we knew so little, there was a tendency to be somewhat cautious — an inclination to put our best foot forward.

Now we have reached a more natural, uninhibited way together, and we find ourselves especially close. And perhaps it is inevitable that on occasion we may step on each other's feet, leaving the anger of frustration, the pain of disappointment.

I am sorry that I have hurt you and caused you to question my affections, because I love you more than I can adequately say. And I ask your forgiveness, your understanding, and your hand so we can step over this together and allow our love to lead us on.

All my heart ever intends and desires to do is to love you . . . as deeply, as gently, as perfectly as possible.

— Carol Ann Oberg

We've Had Our Share of Difficult Times, but Our Love Is Forever

So many relationships end these days
because people are afraid to make
    a commitment.
They expect perfection,
and when it doesn't come
or the least little problems occur,
    they're ready to say it's over.
Thank goodness we never
    let that happen to us.
We've seen difficult times,
    we've had our troubles,
        we've shared heartaches
            and disappointments.

I'll be the first to admit that
    I'm not perfect,
and I think you'd be willing to admit
    that neither are you.
But what keeps us together
is the fact that we care enough . . .
    about the commitment we made,
      the life we planned for
        and built together,
          and the love we've always
          known.
We're among the lucky ones . . .
    we've found a love
      that is forever.

             — Anna Marie Edwards

I Hope You Can
Forgive Me for Hurting You

What I have to say is simple:
I'm sorry.
I know sometimes
I can be insensitive,
and I do things without thinking.
But I would never
intentionally hurt you,
and my heart is heavy
knowing I have been
the source of pain for someone
who means so much to me.
I hope somehow you'll forgive me,
and that we can go on from here,
stronger than before,
to enjoy the love we share.

— Julie Anne Gridley

More than Anything, I Want Things to Always Be Right Between Us

I wish that loving you the way I do
were all it took to keep things
   right between us,
because loving you comes so easy for me.
But it takes a lot of effort
   to turn good feelings
into a relationship that works.
It isn't always easy
to know what you are feeling,
to know what to say, and what not to say,
to know when you need me to listen,
and to recognize the times when nothing
   needs to be said.

I want to be at your side always,
but what do I do
when it seems that what you want most
is to be alone?

There is so much that I want to do,
   but I don't know if I should,
and this leaves me feeling confused
   and alone
wishing you would understand . . .
that all I really want to know
   is that you know I love you,
      and for you to tell me
         that is enough.

— Garry LaFollette

We may have some problems,
    but one thing is certain . . .

I would rather spend an occasional
    unhappy moment with you
than spend my time on this earth
    without you.
I can't imagine how my life would be
if you weren't here to share it
    with me,
and I know we can get through
    anything together.

— Christine Anne Keller

No Matter What,
I Love You

I often wonder what
made us fall in love
with each other
We are so different
from each other
Our strengths
and weaknesses
are so different
Our ways
of approaching things
are so different
Our personalities
are so different
Yet our love
continues to grow and grow

Perhaps the differences
we have add to the
excitement of our relationship
and I know that both of us
as a team are stronger
than either of us alone
We are basically different from
each other
but we have so many
feelings and emotions in common
And it really doesn't matter
why we fell
in love
All that matters to me
is that we continue
to respect and love
each other

— Susan Polis Schutz

Maybe Someday
There Will Be a Way

I don't mean to
make life harder for you.
But I know
   that I sometimes do.

Maybe someday I'll get better
at dealing with the problems
and avoiding the rough spots
   along the paths
      of our lives.

Maybe someday we'll both
   have more peace and quiet time,
      more serenity and sunshine,
more you and me,
   and fewer outside complications
      taking up our time.

Maybe someday
I'll be able to make it
      easier for you.
   That's one of the things
         — in my life
      and within my heart —
         that I'd like to be able to do.

— Adrian Rogers

You Don't Ever Need to Wonder
About My Love for You

I know that at times
it is very difficult for you
    to understand me;
I know how frustrated you often get.
But please believe me when I say
that the doubts and confusion
    I sometimes feel
are not because of you,
but because of me and the changes
that are beginning to happen
    inside myself.

I have never doubted
    my feelings for you;
I know that they are as strong
    as any bond could possibly be
between two people.
My love for you is strong.
I am becoming more mature,
and with maturity come responsibilities
that I must learn to deal with.
Please don't think
    that I'm dissatisfied with you,
for without you,
an important part of my life
would be missing.
I have come to rely on you;
I need your presence to reassure me
that everything will be all right.
And I need you most of all
because I love you.

— Linda Tillmann

I'm Sorry for the Times
When Things Don't Go
So Well for Us

Whenever things start getting
uncomfortable between us,
our tendency is for each of us
to retreat into separate corners.
But all we find then
   is silence and solitude,
when what we most need to have
   is communication and
      the togetherness of
         two people who care
            about each other.
I'm sorry for the times
when things don't go
so well for us, but please . . .
don't hide away: turn to me
   and let me turn to you,
      and let me remind you
         that through it all . . .
            I love you.

And I want you to know that I do.

— Adrian Rogers

I'm Sorry for Hurting You, and I Promise You All My Love

I promise to give you all my love
for now and forever,
to keep your love close to my heart
so that we will never grow apart.
I promise to confide in you
if I feel insecure.
I promise not to doubt your judgments
or actions, without first listening
to the feelings in your heart.
I promise to support you in everything
you try to accomplish,
because your goals
have become our goals
to achieve together, side by side.

I promise to look back on
the good and bad times
with a smile,
to learn by each mistake
and know that, with every step of success,
we will make it if we just try.
I promise to offer you all the happiness
I am capable of giving you,
to see that the future is ours
to make the best of.
I promise to set time aside
to be best friends,
to dream dreams and make them reality,
and just to say "I love you."
I promise most of all
never to take you for granted,
because you are the love of my life.

— Michele Thomas

ACKNOWLEDGMENTS

We gratefully acknowledge the permission granted by the following authors to reprint their works.

Sharon Leigh Johnson for "We Can Work It Out." Copyright © Sharon Leigh Johnson, 1988. All rights reserved. Reprinted by permission.

Linda Tillmann for "I Hope You Will Always Stay in My Life." Copyright © Linda Tillmann, 1988. All rights reserved. Reprinted by permission.

Anne Marie Holleran for "I Apologize for How I've Been Acting Lately." Copyright © Anne Marie Holleran, 1988. All rights reserved. Reprinted by permission.

Paula J. Lemley for "Thank You for Understanding When I'm Not Perfect." Copyright © Paula J. Lemley, 1988. All rights reserved. Reprinted by permission.

Jane Alice Fox for "I'm Sorry that I Haven't Been Myself Lately." Copyright © Jane Alice Fox, 1988. All rights reserved. Reprinted by permission.

Nanci Brillant for "If Only I Could, I Would Take Back the Hurt." Copyright © Nanci Brillant, 1988. All rights reserved. Reprinted by permission.

Mae Williams for "Let's Be Open and Honest with Each Other." Copyright © Mae Williams, 1988. All rights reserved. Reprinted by permission.

Terry Everton for "I'm Sorry for the Hurt That's Come Between Us." Copyright © Terry Everton, 1988. All rights reserved. Reprinted by permission.

Dawn M. Miller for "Even Though We Have Our Disagreements, I Always Know Our Love Is There." Copyright © Dawn M. Miller, 1988. All rights reserved. Reprinted by permission.

Carol Ann Oberg for "Our Closeness Sometimes Opens Us More to Hurt." Copyright © Carol Ann Oberg, 1988. All rights reserved. Reprinted by permission.

Julie Anne Gridley for "I Hope You Can Forgive Me for Hurting You." Copyright © Julie Anne Gridley, 1988. All rights reserved. Reprinted by permission.

Christine Anne Keller for "We may have some problems, but one thing is certain . . . ." Copyright © Christine Anne Keller, 1988. All rights reserved. Reprinted by permission.

A careful effort has been made to trace the ownership of poems used in this anthology in order to obtain permission to reprint copyrighted materials and to give proper credit to the copyright owners.

If any error or omission has occurred, it is completely inadvertent, and we would like to make corrections in future editions provided that written notification is made to the publisher: BLUE MOUNTAIN PRESS, INC., P.O. BOX 4549, Boulder, Colorado 80306.